Frozen Words

Collection of Memories

Sherny

BookLeaf Publishing

India | USA | UK

Made with ❤ on the BookLeaf Publishing Platform

www.bookleafpub.in

www.bookleafpub.com

Dedication

In loving memory of my mother Celine Joseph
- Flowers reached me beyond the walls with memories of being you beyond the sky.

Preface

I'm Sherny, writing poetry has been an hobby since childhood, but now its a passion.

Acknowledgements

My sincere gratitude goes to my family who has encouraged me to write poetry and being supportive in this process. Your guidance was invaluable. Their believe in my words as poetry was my hope. I am profoundly thankful.

1. A Promise

Be a sacred promise
That seem not to break through
In darkness and light
That seem not distant from heart

In dawn and dusk
That binds clouds and stars
In sickness and need of a soul
That cures beyond meds and sciences

A promise as pious as "prayer".

2. Disguised Armour

Withered by the escastic seasons in charm
Knight stands in an disguised armour unknown
Aloof by the mountain top
Alas, searching for the lost song

Were for with thee
Though shall I pass
Art thee by thine side
Stow shall never pass storm
For thee I unwrite my thoughts

Wondering
Could it be ever more
Appauling than to be in thee
Forever and every fortnight

3. Fading In

This Night is cold in the kingdom
I can feel you fade away
Now, I'm slipping through the cracks of your warm
embrace
So please, could you find a way. to hold me together
through the warmth of your very own heart
Don't let me drag my feet along the
corridor of the making world

Just hold me tight to yourself,
hold me from falling apart
For let me tell you that I was all broken
Once when you found me amidst the
woods in the chilliest of the season
Don't let me sink in the vibes of another soul

Don't let me down from 'love' that was one of the only
reason
to survive, Hold me close to you..forever eternity

4. Lost Love

If you were there
There to see, a lonely emptiness
which was all I saw
Nothing real at all, but still a fiction
you could have seen how your
loved ones broke down in tears of silence

The silence which is filled with sorrow
My ears strained to hear you speak
Everytime there was a call on the
closed door, I ran upto it, thought you
would come calling my name and hug me

But I saw, was a lonely emptiness
Emptiness of the "lost love"
"If you were there" These words
Just words ~ are now beneath sand & water

Everyone is a stranger here..
You were one among the person called "Me"...

5. Departed Sorrow

So much that I lived in you, that you were my shadow
if you were there to see your departure
you must have seen there's more to the world
Than sorrow whether a man is alone
or in company. This is when for the
first time I saw you depart from me
with the dusk to never return back

Life is short, everyone lives it
some enjoy it some just spend it
you are among those who lived each
every moment of life just for your loved ones.

This was the time when a little heart
which was close to you understood that
Life does not stretch to infinity.

6. Believe

That perches in the soul
sings the tune without the words
never stop at all

The sweetest in the gale is heard
I've heard it in the chilliest of land
on the strongest of sea

The waves juz hitting the sea-shore
for returning back and turning with
the magnetic force ever

Earning for belief and faith
Once when the angels came down
beneath heaven to heal the hurt

For frozen lay there the naive
But....

In the grave of tears

7. Strange Grievance

That...At times stuck between the noise of the world
around me and the silence of your grave.
There it is, I hear your voice as the
very first time I recognised you.
The hustle of the wind that said to me
probably, you were an angel
That voice of yours that lasted for an hour of your
existence.

The way you looked within me trying to
shield me against the harsh reality of world
There I was yet looking at you unfolding within myself
trying to relate few unspoken words that was meant to
be you.

That very moment world seemed so strange
Though it was shed with grievance across
uneven faces still they were mocking from within.
I lost you to the heavens.

8. Entreated Seasons

Seasons juz pass through
Amongst the scared & pious
somethings that doesn't change is Me
I ever miss you more

I juz touch myself and feel you more close
to me, this is how I love you.
I can feel you through miles apart
I can hug you, hold you the way as
your own soul beholds you.

Juz wanna say love is beyond the stars &
sky to prove it, entreated by you trust.
I'm all yours by faith, don't lemme 'die' without being
'you'

Juz come & hold me through your memories
Forever & ever more I miss you
For all I ever got is your memories
to last within me

9. Soulful Memory

Life is a mere memory
Memory of a living soul
Memory surrounded by rememberance
of the never ending flowing waves

One fine day, lay still on the shore
graved by loneliness and tears
From the beginning of dawn to dusk
Life lay cold and frozen in an alarm

Rememberance burnt down to ashes
Buried in the sorrow of departed life
Leaving rest of the world beyond

We all have to travel death for life
to reach to a new land...
In Memory for lost souls

10. Life Aura

I do not make fake promises
For I ain't a fake heart

I come from a world
A world of my own
beyond by sky
surrounded by stars
guarded by prayers

For there's always a sun-rise beyond sunsets
promising on a tomorrow of faith and love
disguised as mermaid

For the love of waves
living by the aura of sea
Juz sorted by heart
connected through soul

That's me !

11. Me

That was Me
It's always been me
When I look into the mirror of consciousness
I see myself within a realization
That says..

'If you could love and behold
Aid you soul to a complete
strange world then why not
behold yourself with the same hands'
so that's to the universal call

That aint gonna me neverthless
It's juz me
And there's not gonna be another "Me"

12. Being You

Oh ! I just realised that you are more than a dream
Though I'm close to you, yet I can feel the distant
I know you have a different heart and its already taken

Yet ma heart ain't distant from you
It's all me..It's juz in me !
May be a distant road, but yet I feel
Your love in me has cured me against all the odds

I wanna secure my love too and only
you could take care of the person in you
Coz I wanna like you to be the same as
long as my breathe takes me to survive

Juz promise me down the road
you will yourself never seem to be far
to become someone else.
Juz like now, be more the same as your now
- forever now.

13. Speaking Words

Eyes speak louder than words
so if you could reach me
hold me close to your heart
speak to me just one more time
This time I promise to hear and be by your side

I would forever have faith in you
I will forever, just have your trust on me
Love me the way you do love
Just want to see you once

All I wanna say - "I miss you more"
Look into my eyes & you would
know my pain, just for a fortnight
hug me close to your soul
Could you just be with me for a fortnight
that would last forever

14. Twinkling Tales

Can you just be more than a dream
Though I'm close to you
Yet I can feel the distance

I know you have a different heart
But my heart ain't distant from you
I know its all me still all I want you to do
is take care of the person in you
Coz I love you too close and
would like you to be the same
as long as my breathe takes me to survive

Your love had cured me against all odds
I wanna secure my love to
And only you could take care of the
angel in you..

Just promise me down the road you would never
seem too far anybody else
Just like now be more the same forever more.

15. Finding You

I'm gonna play a song that you may have never known
anyway I'm just gonna sing and play
fading in, fading out on the edge of life
I was in pain but you were my cure
you were my place of peace
my existence is you even though you faded away

You became an unknown fear;
fear of not existing anymore
hope you can hear my unsaid words

Every tear was a hope that you are there for me
you can beseech my heart
and touch my worrying soul
My wish upon the stars is deep
so is my love for you
for the reason unknown to me

I am still searching you in my tears and pain
alas ! you reach me to be forever you

16. Re-Birth

From the land of distinct souls
the magic spell bound once again
raising the spirits high in grace
calling in my guarding angels
to look after me, to protect me
against the deceiving world
A world that mocks at me

For my innocent eyes always keep searching you
you were my only peaceful space
you were my home with prayers
a scared lamp which lit my world

If only I could change the fate
If only the lines of my palms could be
written against the words

This time not as your princess
As your warrior...

17. Forever You

I wanna you know that I need you to sing it again
coz you took me back in times when I was broken
I swear that every word you sing
you wrote them for me

I know you never saw me when the lights came in
I'm on my own, will you be there to sing it again
yet from another world
Reach me beyond the clouds
hold me close to your heart
lets match the rhythm

I know you wouldn't let anyone hurt me
I know that things are away from us
the starts wouldn't favour our stories

Yet could I be there in your story
as a part of your very own soul
Could I be ever forever in you !

18. Knight In Disguise

Amidst the meadows of grievances
I stand there beseeching you
banished from my very own kingdom
I search for you in disguise

Wandering if I could ever find you
thither and lost
drowned in tears
your words still reign in me

All I could remember is your last memory
memory of you bidding adieu
I am almost cold in the disguise of knight

My only prayer to find solace in you
I will never depart from you until dawn
neither dusk will keep me away from you

19. Search of You

Lost in the mountains
afraid of the heights
looking all pale and drunk
tired of the tears and screams

Dragging my feet along the ground
still carrying the faith until my last breathe
Until then my search for you continues
amongst the mountains and woods
to find you in a place where we don't have to depart
again

Where the souls are at peace
and they are all happy faces
with no jealousy and hatred around
A place of our very own
that exists in my heart and
reaches you beyond your soul

20. Close To You

Hug me close to your heart
don't let me be seen by the world
hug me close to your soul
don't let me be one among the crowd

Hug me close to your warmth
don't let the dust of deceit surround me
hug me close to your memories
don't let the dawn of hurting words speak to me

Hug me close to your aura
don't let me lie another person in
a world of selfish folks

Hug me close to your prayers
don't let me be dead in the arms of betrayal
Hug me close to you forever
don't let me be lost in the chaos.

21. Be My Eternity

Locked in the mirror of self consciousness
seeking answers for your absence
its been a decade of grief

All I remember is the way your eyes looked at me
hardly does your words ever come across
you are not my forever the saddest part of my life
that you are a memory

A sunny bright day that turned darkness
it was all over, I could see my life scattered
All I could hear was shattering of voices

Each day of your absence has been more grieving within
me
You won't break your promise
you won't give yourself into the dusk
you will always for eternity, be my forever...